AF228475

BABY PIGS

by Martha London

Cody Koala

An Imprint of Pop!
popbooksonline.com

abdobooks.com

Published by Pop!, a division of ABDO, PO Box 398166, Minneapolis, Minnesota 55439. Copyright © 2021 by POP, LLC. International copyrights reserved in all countries. No part of this book may be reproduced in any form without written permission from the publisher. Pop!™ is a trademark and logo of POP, LLC.

Printed in the United States of America, North Mankato, Minnesota

052020
092020

THIS BOOK CONTAINS RECYCLED MATERIALS

Cover Photo: iStockphoto
Interior Photos: iStockphoto, 1; Shutterstock Images, 5 (top), 5 (bottom left), 5 (bottom right), 6–7, 9, 10, 13, 15 (top), 15 (bottom left), 15 (bottom right), 16, 19, 20–21

Editor: Nick Rebman
Series Designer: Christine Ha

Library of Congress Control Number: 2019954951
Publisher's Cataloging-in-Publication Data
Names: London, Martha, author.
Title: Baby pigs / by Martha London
Description: Minneapolis, Minnesota : POP!, 2021 | Series: Baby farm animals | Includes online resources and index
Identifiers: ISBN 9781532167478 (lib. bdg.) | ISBN 9781532168574 (ebook)
Subjects: LCSH: Swine--Infancy--Juvenile literature. | Piglets--Juvenile literature. | Baby pigs--Juvenile literature. | Baby farm animals--Juvenile literature. | Animal babies--Juvenile literature.
Classification: DDC 636.4/07--dc23

Cody Koala

Pop open this book and you'll find QR codes like this one, loaded with information, so you can learn even more!

Scan this code* and others like it while you read, or visit the website below to make this book pop.

popbooksonline.com/baby-pigs

*Scanning QR codes requires a web-enabled smart device with a QR code reader app and a camera.

Table of Contents

Chapter 1

Born in a Barn

Baby pigs are called piglets.

They are born in a barn.

A mother pig gives birth to

ten or more piglets at a time.

They sleep on soft straw.

Watch a video here!

Piglets are **mammals**.
They drink their mother's
milk. Piglets stay close to

their mother. They live with
her in the barn for the first
few days.

Chapter 2

Playtime

Newborn piglets are tiny. But they grow quickly. Piglets play with one another. The mother pig keeps a close watch. She calls out to her piglets if they wander away.

Learn more here!

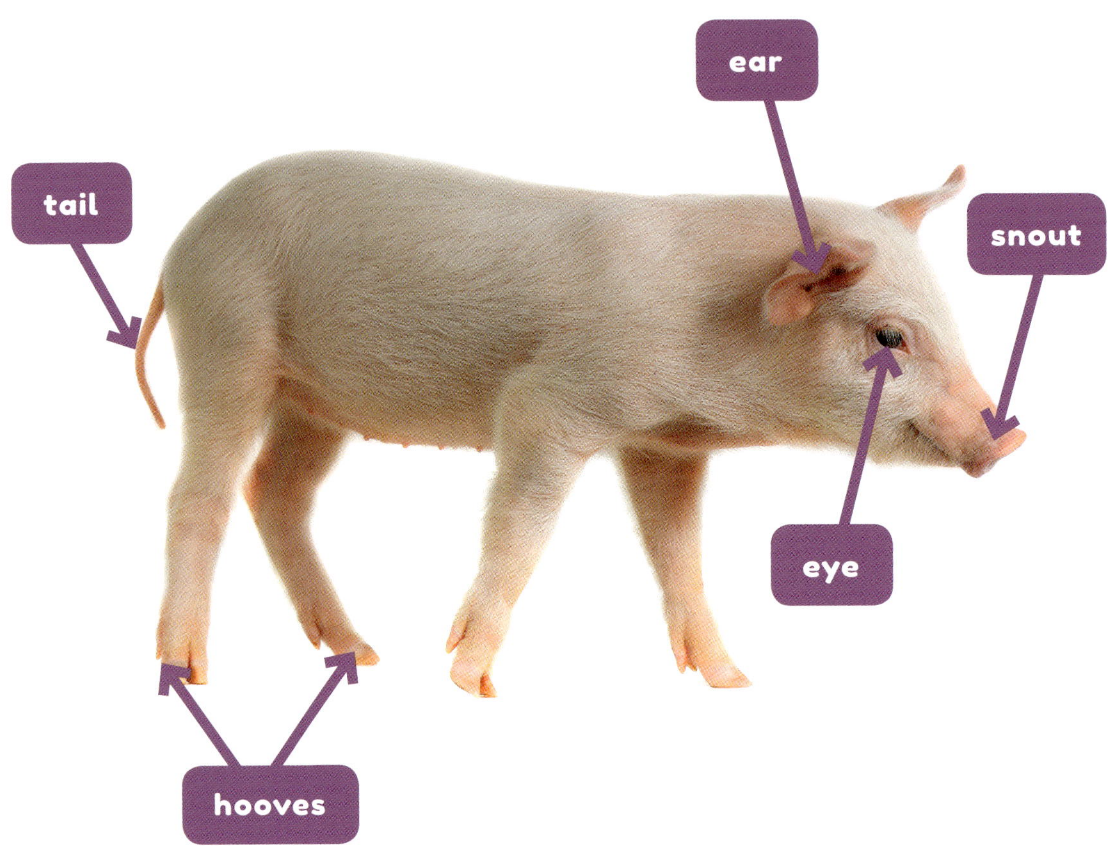

ear
tail
snout
eye
hooves

Piglets have short tails.
They also have short legs.
Piglets' feet are covered
by **hooves**. Piglets have
flat **snouts**. They have an
excellent sense of smell.

Pigs are good swimmers.

Pigs cannot sweat. For this reason, pigs roll around in the mud. Mud helps cool pigs off. It also protects pigs' skin. Pigs do not get sunburned if they are covered in mud.

Chapter 3

Growing Up

Piglets stop drinking their mother's milk when they are three weeks old. This process is called weaning. After piglets are weaned, they eat only solid foods.

Learn more here!

Piglets learn from their mother. She helps them learn which foods are safe to eat. Pigs eat many types of food. These foods include hay, fruits, and vegetables.

A pig's **squeal** is almost as loud as the roar of an airplane.

Chapter 4

Part of a Group

Piglets are **social** animals. They stay in groups. Many pigs live together in large pens. After pigs are grown up, they stay close to the pigs they grew up with.

Complete an
activity here!

Adult pigs need space
to move. They have places
to sleep, eat, and go to the

bathroom. Pigs explore their
pens. Farmers give pigs toys
to play with.

Making Connections

Text-to-Self

Imagine you are on a farm. What would it be like to see a baby pig?

Text-to-Text

What other books about baby animals have you read? How are piglets similar to and different from those animals?

Text-to-World

What might happen if pigs didn't have mud to roll around in?

Glossary

hooves – the hard parts that cover an animal's feet.

mammal – a type of animal that has hair or fur and feeds milk to its young.

snout – the area of a pig's face that includes the nose and mouth.

social – enjoying the company of others.

squeal – a loud, high-pitched call.

Index

Online Resources

popbooksonline.com

Thanks for reading this Cody Koala book!

Scan this code* and others like it in this book, or visit the website below to make this book pop!

popbooksonline.com/baby-pigs

*Scanning QR codes requires a web-enabled smart device with a QR code reader app and a camera.